7-29-74

The President's Commissions

Frank Popper/*Twentieth Century Fund*

KRAUS REPRINT CO.
Millwood, New York
1973

The author, a former staff member of the Twentieth Century Fund, is now a doctoral candidate at Harvard's Government Department. In preparing this study, he interviewed many persons associated with presidential commissions — presidential assistants, commissioners, executive directors, staff members, and consultants. The quotes in this study without direct attribution come from these interviews. The help given by those interviewed is gratefully acknowledged, as is that of Mrs. Elizabeth B. Drew, Washington Editor of the *Atlantic*. The author's wife and several members of the Fund staff contributed valuable comments on the manuscript, and Nancy MacKenzie edited it. The author, however, takes full responsibility for the facts, opinions, and conclusions set forth here.

March 1970

Popper, Frank.
The President's commissions.
Reprint of the ed. published by Twentieth Century Fund, New York.
1. Governmental investigations—United States. 2. Executive power—United States. I. Title.
JK518.P64 1973   353.09   73-12304
ISBN 0-527-71960-9

CONTENTS

1. INTRODUCTION: A SOURCE OF ADVICE

All Presidents need disinterested, expert advice. To meet this need and to supplement the often narrow views of federal agencies, Congress, the press, local governments, and interest groups, Presidents have frequently turned to commissions—*ad hoc,* nonpartisan groups of men not involved in the day-to-day operations of the government.

The most publicized commissions of recent years have been three which President Lyndon B. Johnson appointed in response to crises: the Commission on the Assassination of President John F. Kennedy (the Warren Commission), the National Advisory Commission on Civil Disorders (the Kerner Commission), and the National Commission on the Causes and Prevention of Violence (the Eisenhower Commission), the last of which finished its work nearly a year after President Richard M. Nixon had taken office. In the absence of crises, Mr. Johnson also appointed lesser-known commissions on more technical topics, such as medical manpower and postal service. Mr. Nixon has already appointed and received the report of the Commission on an All-Volunteer Armed Force and has announced plans for commissions on home rule for the District of Columbia, world trade, population growth, and school finance. Appendix 1 lists all the commissions appointed in the last twenty-five years. All recent Presidents have used commissions, but this appendix shows that Presidents Truman, Johnson, and, to date, Nixon have sought advice from commissions more often than President Dwight D. Eisenhower and President Kennedy.

This study describes and evaluates the special presidential commission as an institution of the American political system. It concentrates on what sort of advice can be expected of commissions and why the advice of some commissions has had more impact—in terms of presidential action, legislation, and headlines—than that of others. The study then compares presidential commissions with their best-known foreign counterparts, the royal commissions of

1 ∗

Great Britain. Finally, and partly as a result of this comparison, the study makes recommendations to improve the future operations and advisory capabilities of presidential commissions.

The last study of any length on commissions, *Presidential Commissions* by political scientist Carl Marcy, was published in 1945. Marcy wrote that commissions are "governmental devices of increasing importance. Presidents rely on them more today than in the past. Their activities are news and their findings may profoundly affect the life of the nation. . . .Presidential commissions, as instruments of government, have not received the attention that their importance and influence warrant. Studies of such commissions have been sporadic in appearance and incomplete in context. The few articles on this subject have usually been motivated by the creation and activities of a particular commission."

Since 1945, commissions have remained important sources of advice. Presidents have also used other means to obtain unbiased outside advice. Private task forces gave Presidents-elect Kennedy and Nixon background information and legislative suggestions before their inaugurations. White House conferences, such as the recent one on Food, Nutrition, and Health, have occasionally been held to discuss national problems. The permanent congressional committees, the sometimes confidential executive branch committees, and the highly technical commissions appointed by Congress have all been used to review policies and suggest legislation. But none of these advisory mechanisms are really comparable to the presidential commission. None are so prestigious, none involve such massive effort, none deal with such broad problems, and none so publicly advise the President. Indeed, no other advisory mechanism of the American government can be considered a true alternative to the presidential commission.

All commissions bring together eminent persons to study an issue of national importance. Most commissions are created by Executive Order of the President and are financed by the Emergency, Executive, or Special Projects Funds, all appropriations which can be spent as the President wishes.

When these funds are lacking, commissions can be created and financed by legislation which Congress routinely passes at the request of the President. (In the last few years, commissions have cost a total of about $10 million a year.) Commission members are asked to submit a report containing recommendations for presidential action and legislation by a specific deadline, usually six months to two years later, after which the group disbands. The recommendations are by no means binding, and the President is not even obliged to release the report to the public. However, he almost always does and, once released, copies of the report are available through the Government Printing Office.

The commissioners, headed by a chairman and chosen by the President and the White House staff, are well-known, busy people, some of whom are unable to attend all the meetings. The chairman and the White House staff select a full-time executive director to supervise the daily operations of the commission. He, in turn, recruits a full-time staff, usually composed of young lawyers and government employees. The staff does the detailed work, and a commission that meets three days a month is considered extremely hardworking. The commissioners, among whom the chairman is usually no more than first among equals, provide broad but definite guidance, and the director provides more specific guidance. The staff does some research, contracts for additional research by outside consultants, organizes commission meetings and hearings, and writes drafts of the commission's report. Once the staff has produced a report acceptable to the commissioners, the report is sent to the President.

No complete history of presidential commissions has ever been written, but they date back to the administration of George Washington, who appointed a commission to try to settle the Whisky Rebellion, a 1794 uprising of Pennsylvania distillers against the federal liquor tax. Most nineteenth-century Presidents sought the advice of commissions—Van Buren, for example, appointed one to get information on European postal systems—but the extensive use of commissions for substantive policy guidance began with Theodore

Roosevelt. Apparently inspired by the example of Britain's royal commissions, and wishing to make his actions more palatable to Congress, he appointed a number of commissions: one, the Aldrich Commission, made recommendations which led to the establishment of the Federal Reserve System. After Roosevelt showed the usefulness of presidential commissions, his successors resorted to them more frequently. The recommendations of President William Howard Taft's Commission on Economy and Efficiency led to the creation of the Federal Budget and Bureau of the Budget. Herbert Hoover made extensive use of commissions; his most notable commissions studied Law Observance and Enforcement (the Wickersham Commission), and Recent Social Trends. (Hoover himself was the chairman of two influential commissions on government organization appointed by Presidents Truman and Eisenhower.) Franklin D. Roosevelt's most influential commission was the Brownlow Committee on Administrative Management, the adoption of whose recommendations established the modern, heavily staffed structure of the Office of the President.

Since Franklin Roosevelt's time, as Appendix 1 indicates, Presidents have relied on commissions, and subsequent sections of this study discuss the nature and results of such reliance. The many commissions of the last few years have examined problems and used methods no different from those of their predecessors—recent commissions have been distinctive only in number and in the publicity which a few received. Commissions will continue to be important, but the commission as an institution is a largely unexamined and unevaluated advisory device of the Presidency.

2. THE PRESIDENTIAL INTENTIONS

Presidential commissions are by no means subservient to the President, yet commissions do not operate in a political or administrative vacuum. Presidents do not establish commissions to hear unrelieved criticism of their own policies. Thus, Robert Kennedy's proposal to President Johnson that he, Kennedy, be appointed chairman of a commission to evaluate the conduct of the Vietnam war was not adopted.

Why, then, do Presidents create commissions? Why do Presidents, having many alternative sources of advice both inside and outside the government, turn to commissions? What makes commission advice distinctive? The evidence suggests that there are four major presidential intentions behind every commission: to show concern about a problem, to educate the nation, to get new policy ideas, and to mobilize support for presidential programs.

Often a President acknowledges the public's concern about a problem by expressing his own concern. In creating a commission to study a problem, the President is not obliged to accept the commission's advice or to do anything at all about a problem that may appear to be soluble but often is not. There are times, however, when a President must make a gesture, meaningful or not, to inspire or restore national confidence by showing that he is aware of public distress. Thus, the Eisenhower Commission was appointed in 1968 after Robert Kennedy and Martin Luther King were assassinated, the Kerner Commission after the Newark and Detroit riots of 1967, and the Warren Commission after President Kennedy's assassination in 1963.

But the concern which commissions evidence need not be in response to such clearly traumatic events. Technical commissions enable the White House to show the general public—or, more often, specialized groups—that a problem is being closely watched. Some of these problems are not easily solved, and it is not surprising that the same topic has been studied by more than one presidential commission. Urban

9

affairs, race relations, government organization, poverty problems, trade policy, the medical, legal, and education systems, the draft, and the special status of the District of Columbia have all been examined by several commissions.

However, commissions have *not* studied foreign policy or military strategy. Presidents consider these subjects too sensitive to entrust to a group as public and as independent as a commission. Presidents generally assign such matters to confidential executive branch committees. This is another reason why Robert Kennedy's commission on Vietnam was improbable, and why a commission, suggested by Hubert H. Humphrey and by Senator John C. Stennis of Mississippi on the alleged massacre at Mylai, is unlikely to materialize.

Any commission intended to reflect public concern is always politically risky for a President. Critics can always accuse him of stalling or of making empty gestures. If the subject under study explodes into the news before the commission submits its report, or before action is taken on the report, the commission will seem a weak palliative and criticism will appear to be justified. All commissions, and particularly the highly publicized ones, are intended to show presidential concern, but Presidents, in creating commissions, also have more realistic intentions.

Presidents may intend commissions to educate the nation. Commissions can perform a genuine public service by collecting facts and opinions on a national problem and by summarizing all this information in a coherent and accessible form. Critics may feel that commissions propagandize, but commissions do alert and inform the public. Commercial editions of the reports of the well-publicized commissions have sold many millions of copies. The idea of income maintenance—endorsed four years ago by the Technology Commission—has since become part of public discussion, and of President Nixon's proposals to Congress. The idea was, indeed, the subject of a Johnson-appointed commission which reported to President Nixon in November 1969, and recommended a "universal income supplement program" providing a minimum annual income of $2,400 for a family of four. The Commission also clearly demonstrated the

10

falsity of the belief that the poor are malingerers.

Sometimes a commission report does not please the President. President Johnson, for example, was unhappy about the apocalyptic tone of the Kerner Commission's report and asked the Eisenhower Commission to re-examine ghetto riots, partly because he believed the Kerner Commission had ignored the civil rights progress which had taken place. But the Kerner findings, and especially the concept that white racism could lead to two separate American societies, now are public knowledge and cannot be minimized.

Presidential commissions can educate by stirring up the federal bureaucracy, by being objective monitors and tactful goads to the agencies whose work they examine. The report of the Urban Problems Commission, for example, criticized the Department of Housing and Urban Development's cautious policies on mass-produced housing, and these criticisms led to the new experimental program, Operation Breakthrough. The findings of presidential commissions, often filtered through similar state commissions reporting to governors, city commissions reporting to mayors, and county commissions reporting to county executives, can educate local agencies. The report of the Commission on Law Enforcement and Administration of Justice emphasized that law enforcement, especially on the local level, should be a single coherent system rather than an assortment of independent police, judicial, and corrections agencies. Many states, cities, and counties are now trying to unify law enforcement systems, and a commission flow chart showing the interactions of law enforcement agencies has become standard in police, criminal law, and criminology texts. Clearly, the educational aspect of presidential commissions should not be underrated.

The third major presidential intention is to get new policy ideas. Presidential staff members always maintain that commissions are created to provide the President and the rest of the executive branch with original proposals for action and legislation. However, there is no evidence that commissions attain this goal. For example, the Kerner Commission's major

11

recommendations—expanded social programs for urban ghettos—were not new to many Americans. They were not even new to commissions: the Law Enforcement, Crime in the District of Columbia, Selective Service, Rural Poverty, Health Facilities, and Technology Commissions had already made many of the same proposals, and the Urban Problems, Urban Housing, Income Maintenance, and Eisenhower Commissions made them later.

The apparently radical recommendation of a lesser-known commission, the 1968 Postal Organization Commission — that the Post Office be reorganized as a public corporation, the office of Postmaster General be dropped from the cabinet, and the appointment of local postmasters removed from congressional patronage—had already been proposed by the then Postmaster General Lawrence O'Brien and by an internal Post Office study. These recommendations were subsequently supported by both of O'Brien's successors, Marvin Watson and Winton Blount, and Presidents Johnson and Nixon have proposed legislation adopting these recommendations.

As a rule, commissions do not produce new ideas, and presidential assistants concede that the unpublicized and less prestigious executive branch committees usually produce more new policy ideas than commissions. Sociologist Nathan Glazer, in an article entitled "On Task Forcing" in the Spring 1969 issue of *The Public Interest*, described the intellectual climate of preinaugural task forces, and his description applies just as well to presidential commissions: "The task force collects notions—good, bad, and indifferent—from its members. Some have been around for a long time and never tried—they may have been in reports of the task forces four years back, and even eight years back—and some are being tried on a small scale, and some are being tried somewhere in the recesses of the government and the task force doesn't even know about it (but that's not too likely). And the ideas come from everywhere. . . . The task force is like a huge broom—it picks up all the ideas that are around, does some brief and crude initial evaluation, and puts it down in its report."

12

Task forces, committees, and commissions may not come up with new proposals, but they do make old ones more respectable, plausible, and thinkable. This latter effect is the fourth and most effective presidential intention for seeking advice from a commission—to mobilize support for presidential programs. Commissions may not provide new ideas, but they are an excellent means of publicizing existing ones and giving them legitimacy. A commission presents a broad, national, authoritative, nonpartisan coalition behind its recommendations. This coalition need not rouse its constituencies; it just has to exist. As Thomas (Mike) Gorman, executive director of President Harry S. Truman's Health Needs Commission in 1952, said in a 1967 speech: "Through this type of study, you develop the facts, you involve a great number of organizations previously not interested and you hopefully create a militant consensus in support of the findings of the commission. The report is the foundation stone of legislation and it provides an obvious answer to the familiar myriad of charges raised by hostile legislators—you didn't study the problem long enough, your conclusions were hastily drawn, you didn't consult a broad enough segment of professional groups or of the American people at large."

The membership and the research of commissions are particularly suited to the presidential intention of mobilization. Joseph A. Califano, formerly President Johnson's chief assistant for domestic affairs, told Jack Rosenthal of the *New York Times* that the Income Maintenance Commission "was not set up because we had any doubts that income maintenance was necessary. It was because we had to get sophisticated data and to try to get blue-chip, prestigious commissioners on the line for something that was highly radical at the time." (See Rosenthal's "Study Panels Flourish in Capitol" in the *Times* of December 15, 1969.) In creating the All-Volunteer Armed Force Commission, President Nixon clearly had a similar intention.

Commissions are primarily useful to a President because they can make attractive to the public and to Congress policy ideas that may have been confined previously to special groups. A volunteer army and income maintenance are

13

examples, and the latter shows that commissions can pass ideas to the people across Presidencies. Although the linkage between commission recommendations and congressional approval, popular support, and presidential action may not be direct, a President can often hasten the implementation of an idea by appointing a commission on it. Crystallizing ideas so as to mobilize support for them is what commissions do best, and they do it as well as any mechanism in the American political system.

3. THE COMMISSIONERS

Every commissioner represents a constituency. He may combine constituencies, but a commission generally includes at least one businessman, labor leader, lawyer, educator, editor, farmer, woman, Negro, Protestant, Catholic, Jew, Easterner, Midwesterner, Southerner, Westerner, federal government official, state government offical, city government offical, Congressman, member of a previous administration, enlightened amateur, and friend of the President. This iron law of presidential appointment exemplifies what political scientist Theodore Lowi, in *The End of Liberalism*, called "interest-group liberalism": representatives of major sectors of American society participate, collectively, in arriving at consensus on policy.

Few commission appointments are political plums; if they were predominantly partisan, all presidential intentions and all commission advice would be discredited. In fact, Presidents make scrupulous efforts to achieve bipartisan balance on commission rosters. The chairman of a commission often differs from the President in party affiliation. For example, President Johnson appointed Milton Eisenhower, brother of the late President, to head the Violence Commission. A chairman from one party may be counterbalanced, as Eisenhower was, by a vice-chairman from the other party.

In addition to bipartisan balancing, there is bicameral balancing, that is, an equal number of Senators and Representatives. Bicameral balancing, combined with bipartisan balancing, means that if Congress is to be represented at all, there will be one Democratic Senator, one Democratic Representative, one Republican Senator, and one Republican Representative. Congress will be represented on any commission likely to have great political impact; the Warren, Kerner, and Eisenhower Commissions each had four Congressmen. There is, however, no evidence that commissions with Congressmen lead to legislation more often than commissions without them.

15

Commissioners take seriously their independence from the President. They know that they are to represent specific groups, but they are also conscious of the national interest. They believe that they can reconcile the interests of their various groups with the interest of the nation as a whole. They believe that clashes between the opinions they represent are constructive: they consider the collective advice of a commission valuable to the President and the public because such advice, even if not particularly innovative, represents an honest synthesis of varying opinions. A man who has served on several commissions said, "You know who you're supposed to represent as soon as you see who the other commissioners are. The commissioners are a deliberate cross section of people with lines into other people. But even if you're a delegate, you try to relate to broader interests, including the general public's and the President's." All these views are clear expressions of interest-group liberalism.

Presidential staff members often take pride in the delicate political, regional, racial, religious, ethnic, and occupational balance of commission rosters. The members of a typical commission—President Johnson's Selective Service Commission, which was appointed in 1966—are listed and briefly described in Appendix 2. Three friends of the President—James H. McCrocklin, George E. Reedy, and Warren G. Woodward—were perhaps one over the normal quota, indicating Mr. Johnson's concern about the group's deliberations. The doctors on the commission were demanded by the topic.

If a technical commission's topic is of interest to certain specialists, then they will be heavily represented on the commission. The Health Facilities Commission appointed in 1967, for example, had five doctors, four public-health workers, two lawyers, one governor, one labor leader, one contractor, and one foundation official. If a particular profession is to be heavily represented, then commissioners are appointed to represent the different interests and approaches within the profession. The five Health Facilities doctors were: a health columnist and official; a college health director and former president of the American Medical

16

Association; a pediatrician and medical school dean; a clinic director and researcher; and a general practitioner. The four public-health workers were: a state official; a president of a large city hospital; a health official of the U.S. Catholic Conference; and a chairwoman of a nursing department.

Most commissions have between fifteen and twenty-five members. The smallest commission recently was the Warren Commission with seven members; the largest was the Food and Fiber Commission with thirty-one. These variations in size are significant. The commissions that seemed likely to have political impact were small: aside from the Warren Commission, the Kerner Commission had eleven members and the Eisenhower Commission thirteen. These smaller commissions could meet often, work hard, reconcile their differences, and issue a report quickly; the Kerner Commission finished its work five months ahead of its deadline. The larger commissions generally had longer periods of time in which to operate. Commissions dealing with technical topics where only a small number of constituencies had to be represented were small—Narcotics and Drug Abuse had seven members, Crime in the District of Columbia had nine, Postal Organization ten—and also had short deadlines. If a specialized topic demanded the representation of many interests, the commission was large and had a distant deadline. For example, the Food and Fiber Commission, asked to evaluate agricultural and related trade policies in twenty months, was large because, in addition to the customary political, regional, ethnic, religious, and racial representation, it also had to represent different intellectual approaches to agronomy, agricultural products (cotton, grain, livestock, wool, tobacco, and dairy products), and economic interests (small farmers, large farmers, cooperatives, unions, agricultural finance, food-processing and farm-machinery companies).

The most striking feature of commission rosters is that the same names appear again and again. In the last twenty years, during which time Republican and Democratic Presidents have held office for approximately equal periods, seven persons have served on three commissions (see Appendix 3). Twenty-five other persons have served on two commissions
2

(Appendix 4). Of these thirty-two persons:

25 were appointed by Democratic Presidents
23 of the 25 were appointed by President Johnson
1 person served only under Republican Presidents
6 served both Democratic and Republican Presidents.

Under President Johnson, six of the thirteen members of the Technology Commission served on at least one other commission; so did eight of the twenty Selective Service commissioners and seven of the twenty-one Income Maintenance commissioners. This trend has continued under President Nixon; five of the fifteen members of the All-Volunteer Armed Force Commission have been commissioners before. The highly publicized commissions tend to have less overlap than other commissions, but at least 10 per cent, and often 25 per cent, of the membership of any commission has served before or will serve again on another commission.

Commission members do not form a clique, but, with their other public responsibilities, with their access to print and publicity, and with their positions, directorships, awards, club memberships, and honorary degrees, they are more like each other than they are like their constituents. They know, or know of, each other. They are primarily administrators, and they are used to working in committees. They have already succeeded in their careers, and their commission service is an honor rather than a steppingstone. They do not really need the nominal payment they get for their commission service. Some have national power, and all share what may be called the conservatism of personal success. They are all accustomed to having their advice sought.

In an article entitled "Government by Commission" in the Spring 1966 issue of *The Public Interest*, sociologist Daniel Bell, a member of the Technology Commission, observed: "The distinctive virtue of the Government Commission is that there is a specific effort to involve the full range of elite or organized opinion in order to see if a real consensus can be achieved." However, important groups of "organized opinion" are consistently underrepresented on commission rosters. Young people are such a group. The youngest commissioners—Vernon Jordan on the Selective Service Commission, Senator Fred R. Harris of Oklahoma on the Kerner Commission, and Clifford Alexander, former chairman of the permanent Equal Employment Opportunity Commission, on the Income Maintenance Commission—are generally in their thirties, although Stephen Herbits, on the All-Volunteer Armed Force Commission, was in his late twenties and was appointed specifically to represent youth. Most commissioners are, at the time of their appointment, in their fifties and sixties, and about as many are in their seventies as are in their thirties. However, youth is heavily represented on commission staffs.

There are not many Americans of Mexican, Italian, Slavic, Oriental, Puerto Rican, or Indian descent on commission rosters. Americans who were born abroad are rare, and poor Americans are rarer. The educators on commissions tend to be administrators—deans and presidents—rather than teachers, although many professors serve as consultants. Educators from primary and secondary schools are few. Nearly all commissioners hold college degrees, and many have advanced degrees. As political scientists Thomas E. Cronin and Sanford D. Greenberg wrote in the introduction to their collection, *The Presidential Advisory System,* commissions and other advisory mechanisms are "extraordinarily skewed in composition in favor of the best educated and the professionally well established." There are not many women on commissions; and since nearly half these women are black, black women, who combine two constituencies, are better represented than white women. Most important, groups generally judged extremist or illegitimate are not represented at all: H. L. Hunt, Dr. Benjamin Spock, and Stokely Carmichael have no chance of becoming commissioners. Commission advice comes from a consensus of mainstream, prosperous, unalienated individuals, who represent well-defined constituencies interested in pragmatic reform rather than ideological reaction or revolution. All these commission characteristics are consistent with interest-group liberalism.

In making up a roster, presidential staff men are aware

19

of the features of American political life described in this chapter. One Johnson aide recalls: "After we had a topic, we'd make up a list of the general skills and areas we wanted represented, but no names. The lists were a lot alike. We'd check with the appropriate departments, the Budget Bureau, and the Civil Service Commission. They'd suggest specific names which would go to the President. He would add, subtract, or substitute names or categories. He'd add the people we wanted for general wisdom—at-large delegates. When he didn't like a list, he'd say things like, 'That guy's been on everything lately,' or, 'Everyone's from New York and Texas. See if you can spread it out a little.'" This aide's statement illustrates interest-group liberalism in action.

Then the presidential staff would telephone the people on the lists and, according to the aide, "We had no trouble getting people to serve; we'd dealt with some of them before, and they were all flattered. Even if they didn't agree with us on, say, Vietnam, they'd agree to join. I think the reason was that people believed the President read the reports and paid attention to the recommendations. They thought they saw a chance to make a difference, I guess, and they jumped at it. We and the chairman would find an executive director by interviewing around Washington; that wasn't hard, either. Sometimes, if the director asked, we'd help him get a staff by getting people detached from agencies. One director told me we'd saved him a couple of months on the telephone. But, most of the time, we'd just sit back and watch the commission. If we had gotten together a slate that was both fair and favorable, we had a pretty good idea of where they would go and what they would say." But before examining where they go and what they say, the role of the staff should be examined.

4. THE STAFF

The staff has three components: the executive director, the subordinate staff, and the consultants. Executive directors, chosen by the White House staff and the chairman, are responsible for the daily operations of commissions and are not subject to the guidelines controlling the appointment of commissioners. They are usually younger and less well known than the commissioners, and they have more professional knowledge of the commission's topic. Charles Bishop, an economist, directed the Rural Poverty Commission; James Vorenberg, a law professor, directed the Law Enforcement Commission; and doctors directed all the recent medical commissions. If a commission is likely to have a major political impact, a lawyer with Washington, that is, political, experience will be appointed director. David Ginsburg, a partner in the Washington firm of Ginsburg and Feldman, directed the Kerner Commission; Lloyd Cutler, a partner in the Washington firm of Wilmer, Cutler, and Pickering, directed the Eisenhower Commission; J. Lee Rankin, U.S. Solicitor General from 1956 to 1961, directed the Warren Commission. For executive directors, commission work is usually a step forward in their careers.

The director's first task, for which the commissioners customarily give him a free hand, is the recruitment of the subordinate staff—generally about thirty people, including nonprofessionals. The number of commissioners has nothing to do with the size of the staff. The size of the staff of some technical commissions, even ones with many members, has been constrained by financial, and thus political, limitations imposed by Presidents. The thirty-one-member Food and Fiber Commission could only afford a staff of seventeen. President Kennedy's seven-member Narcotics and Drug Abuse Commission had a staff of eleven, his eleven-member Registration and Voting Participation Commission a staff of seven, and his nine-member Campaign Costs Commission a staff of five. All of these commissions were given the

2 *

relatively small sum of about half a million dollars, approximately the cost of an executive branch committee. The fact that some technical commissions have a small staff often means that the President does not really want much substantive advice from them; he is doing little more than showing concern for a specialized group. If he had wanted more from them, he would have given them more money to hire larger staffs. Such funds are given to the small, highly publicized commissions from which he expects broad political impact. Both the Eisenhower and Kerner Commissions had more than a hundred staff members, and the Warren Commission had over eighty; each of these commissions reportedly spent more than $2 million. Other commissions each spent approximately $1 million, about the usual cost of a congressional committee's investigation. On any commission, the staff does most of the work, and if the President expects a lot from a commission of any size, he must give it enough money to hire an adequate staff.

If the staff is to be large, the job of recruiting it can be time-consuming. Lloyd Cutler reportedly spent ten weeks of the eighteen-month life of the Eisenhower Commission lining up a staff. According to executive directors, most people who are approached are honored, just as the commissioners are, but, unlike commissioners, they cannot leave their jobs or are reluctant to accept a job with a short-lived commission. One director who recruited personnel in 1968 felt that disenchantment with United States foreign policy and the presidential campaign caused some younger candidates to turn him down; in any case, commissioners and executive directors are easier to find than staff members.

There is general agreement that the best sources of staff are federal agencies, congressional committees and, particularly for the highly political commissions, Washington law firms. (Nearly all of the Warren Commission's professional staff, as well as all of its commissioners, were lawyers.) As one Technology commissioner said, "The people under forty always seem to be changing jobs, and commission work, although it may not lead to anything, can be fun for a year. There are invisible networks, too. People in Labor, Commerce, and the appropriate committees always know each other and know what peoples' specialties are. They know who is available, and for what price. A director will call up a guy in an agency, and find that the guy mailed him a résumé the day before."

Once the director has hired his subordinate staff, he finds himself caught in the middle between the commissioners and the staff. Commissioners, staff members, and directors all describe commission-staff relations as "acerbic," "tense," and "guarded." In an informative article entitled "On Giving Oneself a Hotfoot: Government by Commission," Elizabeth B. Drew wrote in the May 1968 *Atlantic Monthly*: "The staff is often composed of young, less experienced people who still think the world can and should be changed; the commissioners know better.... So the policy alternatives go up from the staff, and policy directives come down from the commissioners, and seldom do the twain meet, except in the person of the exhausted, whipsawed executive director."

The director must mediate between the commissioners and the staff; if possible, he must unite them. His job can be difficult if the staff ignores the commissioners or if the commissioners ignore the staff. Edward Jay Epstein in *Inquest*, a book highly critical of the methods and findings of the Warren Commission and the most detailed study ever made of a commission, quotes one staff member who commented that the commissioners "had no idea of what was happening." Epstein quotes another staff member who, asked what the commissioners had contributed, answered, "In one word, nothing." Rankin, the director of the Warren Commission, when reluctantly forced to choose between the commissioners' findings and the staff's, generally sided with the commissioners. For example, the staff was suspicious of inconsistencies in the statements of Marina Oswald, the widow of the alleged assassin, but Rankin and the commissioners were not, and their views prevailed. Epstein quotes Rankin as saying that some of the younger staff members "simply didn't understand how a government inquiry worked" and adds that Rankin felt that "the commission,

23

through its experience and collective wisdom, gave the investigation its direction and focus."

On any commission, the executive director must, as one staff member said, be "good at getting compliance or silence from people while pretending to seek their advice." He must prevent commissioners from taking the commission in contradictory or irrelevant directions. He has the nearly impossible task of making commissioners and staff members regard the commission as a cohesive group, and not as a fragmented and temporary collection of individuals. But, above all, he must infuse both the commissioners and the staff with a sense of urgency.

The short life of a commission, rather than simplifying the director's job, complicates it. Much of his work is administrative, unconnected with the substance of the commission's topic. While the staff does research and writes, he recruits, mediates, reassures, badgers, negotiates for secretaries, and argues with the Government Printing Office about how long it will take to print the report. He has little to do with writing the report, and his detailed grasp of the commission's topic—for which he was hired in the first place—is only rarely used.

The deadline also means that the executive director and the staff must hire short-term or part-time consultants to perform essential research. These consultants are usually academics or agency specialists who, because of prior commitments, cannot accept staff jobs. Sometimes the staff hires consulting firms, "think tanks," or polling organizations to do research. Arthur D. Little, Inc., the Cambridge, Massachusetts, consulting firm, did much of the Postal Organization Commission's research, and Louis Harris took several polls for the Eisenhower Commission. The consultants write the technical supplements which may accompany the final report. In their papers the consultants are free to disagree with the findings of the report.

The supplementary work can be important. The Walker Report to the Eisenhower Commission, *Rights in Conflict*, which attributed the violence in Chicago at the 1968 Democratic Convention primarily to a "police riot," is an example

24

of such supplementary work. The Eisenhower Commission also issued supplementary reports on other outbursts of violence in Miami (during the 1968 Republican Convention), Washington (New Left demonstrations when President Nixon took office), Cleveland (a black nationalist gun battle with police), and San Francisco (campus violence at San Francisco State College), as well as reports on protest politics, the history of American violence, media coverage of violence, assassinations, individual violence, law enforcement, and gun control.

The use of consultants by commissions taps otherwise unavailable talent, but the work of the consultants arouses mixed feelings in executive directors, staff members, and commissioners. They all believe that much of the consultants' work is indifferent and does not compare with the research which the same consultants perform in academic life, in their agencies, or in their research organizations. The consultants agree, and many, especially the academic social scientists, feel rushed, uncomfortable, and unappreciated, especially by the lawyers who are likely to staff the highly political commissions. On July 9, 1968, sociologist Amitai Etzioni wrote in the *Wall Street Journal*: "For the social scientist a rush job on a Government commission is more likely to retard his career than to advance it. . . . [Social scientists'] methods of obtaining data are rendered ineffectual because usually the lawyer staff-directors have little of the background needed to work with social scientists, and above all because everyone is in a rush. More than anything else, commissions are part of government by fire-brigade. . . . The facilities and methods under which commissions work would have to be modified if social scientists were to effectively supplement lawyers. Most [commissions] are set up to investigate (in the legislative tradition) and build consensus (in typical committee work), but not to conduct research."

A staff member who was not a lawyer was unsympathetic toward the social scientists: "They asked ridiculous prices, they couldn't produce under pressure, they wouldn't adjust to any kind of bureaucracy, they would tell us they couldn't meet deadlines because they'd been busy picketing, and then they'd just lose interest entirely." Other staff people were more philosophical: "Only about 10 per cent of the consulting work was worthwhile, and I'm not sure we could pick out which 10 per cent. Most of the work was unfocused, irrelevant and gave us no policy help at all. But, then, who were we to ask for instant revelation? Anyway, we always knew what we wanted better than the consultants. We would go to them because we didn't have time to do the work ourselves." Under circumstances such as these, consultants and commissions cannot be expected to work together productively.

The consultants' work, regardless of its quality and its pertinence to the report, is fundamentally valuable to a commission, not for its intellectual merits or policy proposals, but because it involves the appropriate academic, professional, and technical communities in the work of the commission. Just as a President can use a commission most effectively to mobilize broad support for his programs, so a commission can use consultants most effectively to mobilize specialized support for *its* programs—that is, its recommendations. The two strategies are analogous, and differ only in scale. Both are highly deliberate and highly political.

As most consultants, staff members, directors, and commissioners soon discover, the advice which commissions give and the advice which they get is only slightly academic or scholarly; both kinds of advice are far more political. Commissions as institutions should be evaluated in political terms because their operations are primarily political.

5. THE OPERATIONS

At the private meetings of the commission, held in Washington, the commissioners plan, supervise, and review the staff's work. In the last few meetings before the deadline, they review and sometimes revise staff drafts. At these meetings, the disagreements among staff members, among commissioners, and between staff members and commissioners become most marked.

The early meetings are relaxed. Such meetings, often over a weekend for the convenience of the busy commissioners, rarely take place more than once a month. The Kerner Commission had a reputation for hard work, and met for forty-four days over its life of seven months. A more customary pace was that of the Law Enforcement Commission: nineteen days over seventeen months. Eighty per cent attendance, which the small, highly publicized commissions sometimes had, is considered high; some commissions rarely get 50 per cent. (However, some commissioners, if they cannot attend meetings, may send members of their personal staffs to take their place.) The large commissions meet less often and generally have lower attendance than the smaller ones.

Some commissioners have a better reputation than others for useful contributions to commission work. In *Guide to Decision: The Royal Commission*, Charles Hanser wrote that presidential commissions are "far too often . . . characterized less by members willing to sacrifice time to the commission's work than by those willing to accept the publicity of appointment in return for a minimum of effort." Walter Reuther, for example, has a better record than George Meany for attentiveness and attendance. On the Kerner Commission, Senator Fred Harris of Oklahoma and Mayor John V. Lindsay of New York had excellent records, as did U.S. District Judge A. Leon Higginbotham and Patricia Roberts Harris, Howard Law School professor, on the Eisenhower Commission. Whitney M. Young and J. Irwin

Miller also had fine records on the commissions on which they served.

The commissioners who make the most useful contributions are those who have the greatest sense of urgency about the commission's topic. Not surprisingly, many such commissioners are black. Several members of the Technology Commission remember an impressive, three-hour presentation that Whitney Young gave at one of their early meetings. There were one million illiterate Negroes, he said, holding adequate jobs, but living in fear of having their ignorance exposed. Truck drivers, for example, were afraid of being ordered to drive in a strange city, where they wouldn't be able to read the signs on the unfamiliar streets. The unemployment rate for white married men was 2.5 per cent; for black teen-agers out of high school, it was 25 per cent. Black males were "emotionally emasculated" since ghetto schools were geared to educate only black women. He knew the commissions couldn't deliver a miracle, but he emphasized that equal opportunity existed only on paper and in the imagination of daydreamers. Some commissioners maintain that Young's moving presentation decisively influenced all subsequent commission proceedings and the commission's report; so a single commissioner, or a single presentation, can make a difference.

A commission's independence from the President is respected. Once a commission has held its first meeting, executive directors and chairmen are in contact with presidential assistants no more than once or twice a week. Staff members of the Urban Problems Commission reportedly helped draft parts of housing bills even before the commission had reported, but commissions, even those with congressional members, generally have little to do with Congress. Surprisingly, the commissioner who is a friend of the President does not play much of a role in keeping the White House informed. President Johnson's friend on the Kerner Commission, Charles B. (Tex) Thornton, was one of the first members to recognize and emphasize what the commission later came to call "white racism." But usually the friend of the President is on the commission only to remind the other members that they are all, in some sense, the President's men.

28

The White House may show interest in a commission's deliberations on a politically sensitive issue: wiretapping in the case of Law Enforcement, minimum income floors in the case of Income Maintenance, gun control in the case of several commissions, most recently the Eisenhower Commission. Early drafts of a commission's report go to the White House, so that the President and his assistants can keep up to date on the most important stages of the commission's work.

Contact with the appropriate federal agencies, however, is not so casual. Such agencies often assign employees to full-time liaison work with the commission, but the actual amount of cooperation depends on the bureaucratic interests of the agency. "Sometimes, they cooperate too much," said one commissioner. "They want to build empires, get bigger budgets, start new programs, and justify their own existence." More often, agencies feel threatened by commissions, resent them, and tend to give them little help in their work.

Epstein reported that the Warren Commission had "communications problems" with the FBI and the CIA while investigating rumors of Lee Harvey Oswald's possible connections with those agencies. A clearer case of an agency's giving a commission no help involved the FBI and the Law Enforcement Commission. In a December 28, 1969, article in the *New York Times* on J. Edgar Hoover and the FBI, Tom Wicker quoted a participant at a commission meeting describing the behavior of the FBI liaison man, Hoover's assistant Cartha DeLoach: "[He reacted like] Pavlov's dog." Anything that cast doubt on the increase of crime, say a new kind of statistical analysis, DeLoach opposed. Anything in the report about police corruption, DeLoach opposed. Anything that cast any doubt on the statistics of crime, DeLoach opposed. Any notion of a link between crime and social conditions, DeLoach opposed. Fortunately, he pushed just too hard for views like that, and so the FBI wound up with less influence on the report than it might have had because it lost the support of the middle group of commission members."

The relationship between the Selective Service Commission and the Selective Service System was, if anything, worse.

The commission staff requested biographical information on the members of local draft boards, but the then Selective Service System Director, General Lewis B. Hershey, didn't have the information and reportedly was reluctant to ask the boards for it because he thought it would be embarrassing. The commission was able eventually to get the White House to put pressure on Hershey. After all, the President had created the commission precisely because he had, according to a staff member, "smelled something wrong" with the draft: "Hershey resented us, and for a while we only communicated in icy memos."

General Hershey eventually relented and took a survey that revealed that local board members are, in the words of the commission report, "almost exclusively white. . . . Only 1.3 per cent of 16,632 local board members are Negro, 0.8 per cent are Puerto Rican, 0.7 per cent Spanish American. . . . The average age is 58. One-fifth of all the board members are over 70, and of these, 400 are over 80; 12 are between 90 and 99. Almost half have served on their local boards more than 10 years; 1,335 . . . have served more than 20 years." Hershey was right—the information *was* embarrassing: local board members have little in common with the men they draft. The commission recommended, thus far unsuccessfully, that board members serve a maximum of five years and retire after reaching a certain unspecified age. The relationship between this commission and the agency it assessed was exceptionally poor; few commissions have to resort to presidential arm-twisting. Yet all commissioners and staff members emphasize that contact with agencies, especially with agencies that feel they are likely to be criticized in the commission report, can present real problems.

As the commission deadline approaches and the staff writes early drafts of the report, discord within the staff grows. The drafting and redrafting never seem to end, the commissioners seem impossible to satisfy, and the writing always takes longer than expected. The tension described by Amitai Etzioni between the lawyers and the social scientists on the staff becomes particularly acute. In an article entitled "Riot Commission Politics" in the July-August 1969 issue of

Trans-action, political scientists Michael Lipsky and David J. Olson described a process that seems to occur on all commissions when the deadline nears: "Talents perhaps antithetical to those of the researcher are demanded of the staff. These are the ability to work all day and night, the capacity to absorb endless criticism without taking personal affront, and the ability to synthesize the sentiments of commissioners, or to anticipate their sentiments regarding various issues. These qualities are those of lawyers. . . . Those best able to gather and interpret socially relevant data may not perform well in accommodating to the pressures that are brought to bear in writing the final report."

Under such circumstances, the quality of commission research inevitably suffers. Lipsky and Olson wrote: "As individuals with public constituencies, commissioners have to be reassured that their decisions rest upon irrefutable and unambiguous evidence. The time problem intrudes when commission staffs anticipate these needs and try to 'build a case.' . . . Building a case and good research procedures are not necessarily incompatible. But a strain is placed upon mutual satisfaction of both these goals when time is short. Statistics without relevance are collected; time-consuming procedures are honored to make an impression of thoroughness; theories with potential validity are rejected since they cannot be adequately tested. . . . The pressures of time are . . . incompatible with a rational search for answers." Thus, the Kerner Commission, in only seven months, had no time to try to distinguish different kinds of riots or white racism. The Warren Commission's actual investigation of President Kennedy's assassination lasted only ten weeks, but four months were needed to write the commission's report.

The process of writing does more than divide the staff; it produces tension between the commissioners and the staff. Neither side ever has complete confidence in the other. This is inevitable in a situation where the staff submits seemingly endless drafts for the approval of the commissioners. (Some chapters of the Warren Commission report went through twenty drafts.) A journalist who worked with several commissions recalls: "All the strands of activity and hostility always come together in the writing. The first few commission meetings haven't done anything more than introduce the commissioners to each other. They size up each other. Then in the next few meetings, attendance drops off and the staff begins to show its strength. Then the staff trots out its early drafts, and all of a sudden the swing members, the ones with open minds and without ideological preconceptions, assert themselves. They make worthwhile, influential suggestions about the drafts. Apparently vulnerable people like women and clergymen can pull a lot of weight here. Finally, in the last few meetings, the staff produces drafts all over the place, the homework swamps the commissioners, and the staff sneaks in everything they think they can get away with. They get away with a lot, because by this time the commissioners have fourteen chapters to read in two days, and it's too late to change anything anyway."

The similarity between this statement's emphasis on "the swing members" and the emphasis on "the middle group of commission members" in Wicker's quote is significant; the initially uncommitted members can often be the most influential ones. Both statements also suggest that the process of writing the report produces tension between the commissioners even greater than that between staff members, or between the staff and the commissioners. Only in reviewing and revising successive staff drafts must the commissioners choose between alternative interpretations and recommendations. Only in making these choices are they directly confronted with the deep differences among themselves, and among the constituencies they represent. These differences can produce violent arguments and much intrigue.

For example, commissioners can write dissenting footnotes or additions to a commission report, but they often threaten to issue a minority report or to resign from the commission in protest. These threats can be effective, particularly in a highly publicized commission, where a minority report or a resignation, in contrast to an occasional footnote or addition, would be felt to compromise, if not sabotage, the work, prestige, and advice of the commission. An instance of the effective use of the threat of a minority report came late in the work of the Kerner Commission. John Lindsay, apparently fearing that the commission would soften its findings in presenting them to the President, had his personal staff prepare a summary of the report. The summary contained the widely quoted statement, "Our nation is moving toward two societies, one black, one white—separate and unequal." He then threatened to issue the summary as a minority report if the commission did not accept it as *the* summary. Realizing that it faithfully reflected the contents of the report, the commission adopted the Lindsay summary. Generally, though, threats such as Lindsay's are ineffective, particularly if the commission is not in the public eye. The commissioners and staff members seem to recognize that such threats are mostly bluffs, or bargaining ploys.

Commissions operate by consensus, and the consensus can nearly always be made to cover up differences. For example, Epstein reported that the Warren Commission was deeply divided on whether President Kennedy and Governor John Connally of Texas were hit by the same bullet. Three commissioners—House Minority Leader Gerald Ford, former CIA Director Allen Dulles, and former High Commissioner for Germany John McCloy—believed that both men were hit by the same bullet. Three others—Senator Richard B. Russell of Georgia, Senator John Sherman Cooper of Kentucky, and Representative Hale Boggs of Louisiana—believed that the men were hit by different bullets. Because everyone considered a unanimous report vital, a dispute which McCloy described as "the battle of the adjectives" then occurred. According to Epstein: "Ford wanted to state that there was 'compelling' evidence that both men were hit by the same bullet, while Russell wanted to state merely that there was only 'credible' evidence. McCloy finally suggested that the adjective 'persuasive' be used, and the word was agreed upon. . . . The question was thus left open by the Commission."

The dispute here seems to be minor, but Epstein makes a strong case that the Warren Commission's primary conclusion—that Oswald, acting alone, was the assassin—is highly
3

questionable if Kennedy and Connally were *not* hit by the same bullet. By glossing over this problem with a compromise adjective, the commission, in effect, refused to face what Epstein calls "the threshold question" of whether there was more than one assassin. Thus, the search for consensus led to an evasion of the most important problem assigned to the commission and may well have invalidated the commission's work.

On other commissions, the search for consensus can lead to equally disconcerting results. Commission reports never directly criticize the President; indeed, commission reports contain no personal criticism of any kind. No government agency is criticized directly unless its ineptitude or misconduct has been flagrant. No constituency represented by the commissioners is criticized. The Kerner Commission, which so strongly condemned generalized white racism, did not criticize the specific institutions which perpetuated it, was vague on how to eliminate it, and said nothing about whose taxes would have to be raised to pay for the recommended expansions of social programs. The Rural Poverty Commission avoided similar questions. The Eisenhower Commission recommended that national priorities be changed to give social needs primacy over military ones ("While serious external dangers remain, the graver threats today are internal"), but was vague on what kinds of social programs should be enacted and how they should be financed. The Selective Service Commission took no stand on the issues of selective conscientious objection and nonmilitary national service. Similar examples of evasion can be found in the reports of all but the most technical commissions.

However, commissions are not entirely to blame for these evasions. The primary responsibility belongs to Presidents who have asked commissions for answers to politically divisive questions, which commissions operating by consensus cannot, by their very nature, answer. Commissions, as products of interest-group liberalism, simply cannot face up to many of the most important issues dividing the nation. All commissions except the most technical eventually find that they must sidestep vital questions. The goal with which commissioners begin their service—a genuine, constructive synthesis of competing views—is rarely attained. A President may appoint to a commission men with whom he disagrees; the commission's search for a consensus will produce a document without a minority report or a resignation. But this search also seriously compromises the usefulness and the integrity of commission advice.

6. COMMISSION PUBLIC RELATIONS

A commission's private meetings and drafting sessions, important though they are, represent its formal operations; even more important are the commission's public relations, which are intended to educate the public about its subject and to mobilize support for its recommendations. Both these functions carry out presidential intentions in creating a commission. A commission's public relations may also unify the commission by making the commissioners and the staff think of themselves as members of a coherent group. Publicity is more important for the highly political commissions than for the more technical ones, but all commissions devote much time and effort to their public relations. At least until they submit their reports to the President, commissions often lobby for their recommendations. After a commission is formed, there are three major occasions for publicity: the commission's hearings, its interim reports, and the presidential release of its final report.

Most commissions hold public hearings which are roughly similar to congressional ones. The witnesses, who are chosen by the staff and whose expenses may be paid, represent a range of opinions and interests much broader than that represented by the commissioners. Thus, the Kerner Commission heard and questioned such witnesses as Stokely Carmichael, Dick Gregory, and J. Edgar Hoover. The Income Maintenance witnesses included welfare recipients and representatives of welfare rights organizations. Commission attendance at hearings is generally about the same as commissioner attendance at private meetings.

Because commissions are so prestigious, almost all commission hearings receive considerable publicity. Some Kerner commissioners believed that, had they allowed their hearings to be televised live, more riots would have occurred. The hearings of the Kerner and Selective Service Commissions received far more publicity than the competitive hearings of congressional committees. The civil disorders hearings of

Senator John L. McClellan of Arkansas, Chairman of the Permanent Subcommittee on Investigations, focused on possible conspiracies behind riots, on antipoverty workers involved in riots, and on the moral degeneracy of rioters. The Kerner Commission's hearings found no evidence of any conspiracy, no misconduct by antipoverty workers, and no evidence that rioters were the "riffraff" McClellan's subcommittee found them to be—and the Kerner hearings undercut McClellan's.

Similarly, the hearings on the draft conducted by Representative Mendel Rivers of South Carolina, Chairman of the House Armed Services Committee, focused on draft-card burners and found the draft as it existed then (1966-1967) perfectly acceptable. On the other hand, the Selective Service Commission, as a result of its hearings, recommended a number of reforms: drafting younger men (nineteen-year-olds) first, a randomized procedure to determine order of induction within an age group, younger and less entrenched members of local draft boards, simpler and more uniform appeals and administrative procedures, elimination of most student and occupational deferments, and special armed forces training programs to upgrade volunteers who might otherwise be rejected. By 1970, all these reforms had become, or seemed likely to become, national policy, but Selective Service commissioners and staff members believe that their adoption would have been substantially delayed if Rivers's hearings had not been overshadowed by the commission hearings.

Hearings do more than generate publicity. They allow groups not represented on the commission to make their views known. They establish a commission's thoroughness, independence, and impartiality. Most important, there is general agreement, even among commissioners, that hearings inform commissioners so that, by the time the report is being written, their knowledge of the commission's subject is often comparable to the staff's. An Income Maintenance staff member said, "We convinced our commissioners that we hadn't been exaggerating things. Some commissioners had the idea that state welfare programs were more efficient than

3 ★

federal ones, but they couldn't say that after the hearings. We convinced everybody involved that the present system had to be changed."

Most commissions do not need the power, which only Congress can grant them, to subpoena witnesses or to compel testimony. Unlike congressional committees, they do not hear hostile witnesses; instead, they hear representatives of groups interested in influencing the commission's recommendations. Commissions, as Carl Marcy wrote, "are looking not for wrongdoing by an individual, but for some more general facts or trends." The only exception to this rule has been the one commission which *was* investigating "wrongdoing by an individual"—the Warren Commission. At its early meetings, the members, including the four Congressmen, decided they needed the subpoena power, and a few weeks later Congress granted it by a joint resolution. The commission heard 552 witnesses; some, such as Marina Oswald, would not have testified if they had not been subpoenaed.

In addition to hearings, commissions use interim or progress reports to gain publicity. Sometimes these reports are issued because the White House has requested them. In late December 1969, for example, the All-Volunteer Armed Force Commission informally announced the gist of these conclusions—that an adequate all-volunteer military could be created surprisingly quickly and inexpensively—several weeks before President Nixon released its report. The Kerner Commission sent out a series of public letters well before its report was released. The first letter, on August 10, 1967, recommended to the President that he "increase substantially the recruitment of Negroes into the Army National Guard and Air National Guard" and "improve and expand riot control training" in these organizations. The second letter, on October 7, recommended that he "direct the Department of Justice to conduct a series of intensive training conferences this winter for governmental and police officials" concerning "measures for the maintenance of law and order and on programs to improve police-community relations." On February 7, 1968, a letter went to Attorney General Ramsey Clark recommending that he try to persuade local police departments "to provide miniaturized two-way radio equipment for all officers on patrol." The same day, a letter went to Rosel Hyde, chairman of the regulatory Federal Communications Commission, recommending that he "make sufficient frequencies available to police and related public safety services to meet the demonstrated need for riot control and other emergency use."

These four letters contain the only Kerner recommendations that Presidents Johnson and Nixon tried to adopt. The more important Kerner recommendations concerned expanded social programs for urban ghettos, rather than riot control measures, but the prearranged letters allowed the White House to appear publicly to be carrying out major recommendations of the commission. Reportedly, several Kerner commissioners now regret having agreed to issue the four letters and feel that their desire for publicity led them to be manipulated by the White House.

The early release of commission findings and recommendations is not always the result of a White House request. In fact, such early releases sometimes displease the President. President Johnson, for example, was displeased by the Eisenhower Commission's release of the Walker Report on violence at the 1968 Democratic Convention. The commissioners did not mind because they had deliberately issued the report in order to establish their credibility with anti-Johnson and anti-Nixon groups, and they were successful: all their subsequent activities received great publicity. "The Walker Report put us in business," said one staff member.

Once President Nixon took office, the commission was continually in the news. But it was a hold-over commission, it did not deal with a subject of primary concern to the President, and its many public statements could not have pleased him, although he did not comment on them. The commission issued the supplementary research described in Chapter 4; this research totaled fifteen volumes. It issued the four supplementary reports described in Chapter 4 on other outbreaks of violence in Miami, Washington, Cleveland, and San Francisco. In December 1969 these reports led nine Democratic Representatives to urge, unsuccessfully, that

39

President Nixon extend the life of the commission in order that it might investigate the Chicago police raid on the apartment of a Black Panther in which two Panther leaders were killed. The commission issued separate statements of its position on gun control, campus violence, the political power of the police, the historical roots and comparative aspects of American violence, protest politics, individual violence, televised violence, law enforcement, assassinations, violent crimes in large cities, alienation among youth, group violence, and civil disobedience.

Finally, in January 1970, a month after President Nixon had released the final report with no comment, the commission issued a supplementary report on violence and the news media, parts of which could be interpreted as a veiled counterattack on Vice President Agnew's criticism of the media in November 1969. The report stated: "After events are reported, something more is required—opinions, analysis, solutions. These opinions do not always come from the proverbial pillars of the community. . . . Unless we propose to emulate the ostrich, we must expect—indeed the public has a right to demand—that the press will report the day's intelligence, including that which is violent. . . . We must make these points forcefully because we wish to set to one side the querulous contentions of those who see in the press the source of most that is evil and who argue particularly that the press ought to 'accentuate the positive and eliminate the negative.' That may be a good formula for song-writing; in troubled times, as a prescription for news content, it is fatuous." On balance, the Eisenhower Commission's public relations provide a model of how a commission can become noticed even before it submits its report and even though it knows that the President will not carry out its recommendations.

The Eisenhower Commission was clearly exceptional in its public relations; the President's release of its final report generated only a small part of its total publicity. For the majority of commissions, however, the most important part of their public relations comes when the President releases the final report. The commissioners and the staff, despite their previous public relations activities, generally have little to do with the manner of the release; only the President's reaction to the report's advice determines how the report is released. All reports are eventually released, but with varying degrees of presidential enthusiasm. The Warren Commission report was rapidly released in September 1964 to dispel rumors before the approaching election. Legislation based on the Heart Disease Commission recommendations for a national system of patient care, training, and research centers went to Congress so quickly that one presidential staff man told Elizabeth Drew, "In all my experience I never saw a piece of legislation leave the White House on which there was less clarity on what the federal government was going to do." (See her article, "The Health Syndicate: Washington's Noble Conspirators," in the December 1967 *Atlantic Monthly*.)

If the White House is unhappy about a report, release can be postponed. The release of the Rural Poverty report, whose recommendations were estimated by former Johnson assistant Califano in a March 1969 speech to cost an additional $40 billion (about $10 billion more, he said, than the recommendations of the Kerner Commission), was delayed for three months in late 1967. First, the White House told the commissioners and the press, privately and unconvincingly, that release would embarrass the commission's chairman, Edward Breathitt, then Democratic Governor of Kentucky, in the November gubernatorial election. (A Breathitt protégé was running and eventually lost to Louie Nunn.) After the election, the White House maintained that release would cause trouble in Congress for the administration's pending antipoverty bill. The report was finally released when it was discovered that the Government Printing Office had inadvertently sent out several hundred copies to government depositories and libraries. No one had noticed.

The attempt to play down the Kerner Commission report was notably less successful. Early White House leaks before release were apparently intended to weaken the report's impact, but rarely has a public relations decision backfired so badly: press interest was stimulated rather than depressed. When, in late February 1968, advance copies of the report were distributed to the press with notification that the report would not be released for a week, the *Washington Post* indicated that it would not honor the instructions and the release date was moved up three days, thus stirring further media interest. In the end, the media reaction was overwhelming. The *Boston Globe*, for example, had twenty separate stories on the report on Friday, March 1, 1968, and then, on Sunday, there were fourteen more pages on the report. The same day, the television networks devoted eight hours to programs about the report. The report had clearly escaped White House control and found an audience of its own. Subsequent disparaging remarks about it by President Johnson, Vice President Humphrey, and Secretary of Health, Education and Welfare Wilbur J. Cohen only gave the report further credibility with its strongly antiadministration audience.

The release of a commission report is casual if the commission is highly technical or if the White House has lost interest in the topic. The latter happened to the Technology Commission, and in *The Public Interest* Daniel Bell wrote of the February 1966 release of its report: "The commission members had been told that the report would be presented in person, to the President, sometime at the end of the month, and were asked to keep three days open in the middle of the week to come to Washington for the presentation . . . [but] the report was in fact released to the press, in desultory fashion, with no member of the commission on hand to answer questions, and no prior advance notice to the press that the report would be forthcoming—an advance notice which is usually given when the White House wants its press corps to reserve space with its city editors about important stories."

The surest way, intentionally or not, to weaken the effect of a report is to release it during the lame-duck period of an administration. The reports of the Urban Housing and Marine Science Commissions were released between Election Day 1968 and Inauguration Day 1969 because, unfortunately for them, their deadlines were set before President Johnson announced he would not seek re-election. Had he been

42

re-elected, these commissions might have made recommendations important for his new term, but their untimely release appeared to condemn them to oblivion, despite the generally acknowledged competence of their work. "It's just too bad," said one Nixon assistant. "Their reporting during the transition means that the work will only have to be done all over again. But we could never propose legislation to Congress with the reports of Johnson commissions." The aide was correct about transition commissions but not about Johnson commissions: President Nixon, in proposing postal, draft, and welfare legislation to a Democratic Congress, has drawn on the work of the Johnson Postal Organization, Selective Service, and Income Maintenance Commissions. Commission reports which span Presidencies, but which are not issued during transitions, usually get more attention. Examples include President Johnson's Eisenhower and Income Maintenance Commissions, as well as President Kennedy's Registration and Voting Participation Commission. But such commissions are still handicapped.

All commissions need publicity, and all seek it. In order to obtain it, to demonstrate their independence from the President, to seek an antiadministration audience, and to bid for a substantive, long-range impact, a few, such as the Eisenhower or Kerner Commissions, are willing to take the risk of offending the President. No commission does so lightly or happily, but all commissions are highly political and must inevitably compete with other, more partisan political institutions. Their public relations are an integral part of this competition.

7. THE IMPACT OF A COMMISSION

What do Presidents do with commission advice? What impact do commissions have on presidential action, congressional legislation, and public opinion? Assessing the impact of a particular commission is difficult and inevitably somewhat impressionistic. If the President or Congress does not adopt a commission's recommendations immediately, they may still do so later; but if the recommendations are accepted later, the commission's specific impact may be hard to discern. On the other hand, if the recommendations are accepted immediately, the President and Congress may have been ready to accept them anyway; they may have been under discussion for years, and the commission may only have given them the final mark of acceptability. Nevertheless, some generalizations may be made concerning the impact of a commission.

First, a commission that has an immediate impact on policy is likely to be one which deals with a specific, concrete problem. The Warren Commission, beyond its investigative and political functions, also studied the technical problem of protecting the President; its recommendations—to make an attack on the President a federal crime, to coordinate Secret Service and FBI activities more closely, to improve preventive intelligence capabilities and liaison with local law enforcement agencies, to develop new techniques for inspecting buildings, and to increase the Secret Service budget—were quickly adopted. Among the less political commissions, those dealing with technical questions concerning the organization of the federal government—Theodore Roosevelt's on Departmental Methods and on the Monetary System, Taft's on Economy and Efficiency, Franklin Roosevelt's on Administrative Management, Truman's and Eisenhower's Hoover Commissions on the Organization of the Executive Branch of the Government, Johnson's on Budget Concepts—have all seen their most important recommendations put into effect. Commissions dealing with the problems of a limited professional group—the medical commissions, for example, which all recommended greater funding for applied research—have quickly led to presidential action and congressional legislation.

Second, a commission is least likely to have immediate impact on the President or Congress when it deals with a broad problem rooted in the political or social system. Examples are the highly publicized Kerner and Eisenhower Commissions as well as the Law Enforcement, Rural Poverty, Urban Problems, Urban Housing, and Technology Commissions, all of whose major recommendations are unlikely to be adopted soon.

Third, a commission without immediate, specific influence on action or legislation may still have a significant impact within a few years. When the Selective Service Commission reported in 1967, all its major proposals seemed politically unrealistic. But, within a year, President Johnson had curtailed student and occupational deferments, and in November 1969 Congress approved a draft lottery and drafting younger men first. Other commission recommendations are likely to be enacted in coming years. Similarly, the recommendations of the All-Volunteer Armed Force, Income Maintenance, and Postal Organization Commissions would have been considered unrealistic only a few years ago (the Selective Service Commission had even opposed a volunteer army), but these recommendations seem likely to be adopted in the next few years. Presidents Nixon and Johnson have already proposed to Congress legislation based on some of these recommendations. Utopian proposals may not become national policy immediately, but despite changes in administrations, they can still have an impact within a fairly short period.

Fourth, a highly publicized commission which does not lead directly to presidential action or congressional legislation can still have a marked impact on public opinion and discussion if it can find an audience of its own. This audience is likely to be already antiadministration, and the obvious examples are the Kerner and Eisenhower Commissions. Over the long run, the audiences of these commissions may be able to persuade the President and Congress to adopt the commissions' recommendations for sweeping changes in the goals of the nation. However, it should be noted that there are no historical precedents for such commission impact.

Fifth, a commission, particularly a technical commission, generally has no more effect than a President wishes it to have. Commissions are, after all, no more than advisory mechanisms of the Presidency. With the admittedly major exceptions of the Kerner and Eisenhower Commissions, no commission has ever genuinely and publicly escaped from presidential control. And even these commissions, despite their impact on public discussion, have not led the President or Congress to do anything they did not already wish to do.

Sixth, if several commissions make similar recommendations, they may, over the long run, have a combined impact on public opinion far greater than any one of them might have had. Commissions have consistently gone out of their way to recommend stronger gun control laws, the lowering of the voting age to eighteen, expansions of income-support programs and other antipoverty efforts, more coherent urban and migration policies, stronger voting rights and other antidiscrimination measures, draft reform, national social accounts similar to the present national income accounts, a national computerized system to match men and jobs, and less severe penalties for possession of marijuana. Many of these recommendations, which are surprisingly progressive coming from men such as commissioners, are likely to become national policy in the future. A succession of commissions making similar recommendations can have a long-run, cumulative impact.

A common criticism of commissions is that there are never any formal arrangements for "follow-up" or "implementation": commissions are appointed to provide a President with outside advice, but he is not bound to take it, or even to listen to it. "We didn't really learn about our topic until the last few months," said one member, "but then we had to quit, just when we knew the most about it." The above generalizations, particularly the fifth, should suggest that the criticism is misplaced. If the President or Congress wants to pursue a commission's recommendations, they do not need a formal mechanism; if they do not want to do so, no formal mechanism can make them.

At the same time, informal follow-up mechanisms have occasionally been quite effective, at least in the case of the highly technical commissions. For example, the Hoover Commissions obtained considerable follow-up, not only because a privately financed group called the Citizens Committee for the Hoover Report was established, but also because most of the commissioners were already in the government, had been, or soon would be. The members of the influential medical commissions were in positions that allowed them to control medical funding and to arouse their powerful constituencies; these commissions contained many more specialists, more members already located in strategic positions—in the American Medical Association, the medical agencies of the government, the large hospitals, the best medical schools—than the ordinary commission. Informal follow-up was built into these technical commissions.

Informal follow-up for the less technical commissions hardly exists at all, so here the criticism has greater validity. Once their report is written, commissioners and staff members become detached and passive about the fate of their efforts. Commissions function as fairly effective lobbies until they write their report; then, having created a product that might be the basis for further lobbying, they suddenly cease to lobby. No matter what the presidential reaction, commissioners and staff members rarely make any attempt to mobilize support behind their recommendations. Kingman Brewster, President of Yale University, a Selective Service commissioner, reportedly persuaded several Congressmen to vote for the November 1969 draft reform bill, but most commissioners and staff members are not so active. Most consider their function strictly advisory: once they have given the President their advice, they regard him as free to do whatever he wishes with it.

However, of all the less technical commissions, the ones most likely to receive informal follow-up are those highly publicized commissions which escape presidential control.

The Eisenhower Commission has reported too recently for its follow-up to have appeared, but the Kerner Commission's report generated conferences in nearly all the cities that were hit by rioting in 1967; and Mayor Lindsay in New York City, Mayor Walter Washington in Washington, D.C., and then Mayor Ivan Allen in Atlanta, began major evaluations of their cities' programs in light of the standards recommended by the commission. In March 1969, a year after the release of the commission's report, the staffs of Urban America, Inc., and the Urban Coalition, both private groups, produced a highly publicized follow-up to the Kerner report entitled *One Year Later: An Assessment of the Nation's Response to the Crisis Described by the National Advisory Commission on Civil Disorders*, which concluded that "we are a year closer to being two societies, black and white, increasingly separate and scarcely less unequal." Both organizations include several people who worked on the Kerner staff. If informal follow-up to a nontechnical commission occurs at all, it must be the work of staff members and commissioners as individuals. Once the commission's report is written, the commissioners and staff members no longer function as a group.

A technical commission whose advice does not interest the President and which does not quickly get support from an audience of its own will be quickly forgotten. The Rural Poverty report, which appeared only a few months before the Kerner report, made a comparable indictment of American society and government but, unlike the Kerner Commission's, never found a strong constituency of its own and never had a comparable impact. The problems of rural America may, in 1967, have been too alien to city dwellers to be conveyed by a commission report. Still, a fuller explanation for the difference in the impact of the two commissions must take into account the differences in their appointments, operations, and public relations. The Kerner Commission was appointed with greater publicity during a crisis, had a large budget and staff, got considerable publicity for its many hearings, and wrote an apocalyptic report; also, the White House attempt to weaken the effect of the report backfired spectacularly. By contrast, the Rural Poverty Commission

48

was not appointed during a crisis (no rural riots had occurred), had less glamorous members, had a small budget and staff, held only a few hearings and got little publicity, wrote a comparatively understated report, and was the object of a fairly successful attempt at suppression by the White House.

Fortunately, most commissions do not suffer the fate of the Rural Poverty Commission. Groups as prestigious and as public as commissions cannot be completely and consistently ignored, and most commissions eventually have some impact on presidential action, congressional legislation, or public opinion. However, there are still strong constraints on the impact of any one commission.

8. PRESIDENTIAL AND ROYAL COMMISSIONS

The best-known counterpart to the presidential commission is the British royal commission, which has inspired similar commissions in nearly all Commonwealth nations. The comparison between American and British commissions is instructive and can provide some ideas for improving presidential commissions. Presidential and royal commissions treat slightly different subjects. Presidential commissions, as discussed in Chapter 2, do not study foreign policy or military strategy, but royal commissions have treated dominion and colonial topics, as well as logistical problems.

Royal commissions, operating in a comparatively centralized, unitary system of government, often study problems that, in the decentralized and federal American system, are treated by state, city, or county commissions instead of presidential ones. Thus, there have been royal commissions (as well as American state, city, or county commissions) on such topics as gambling, driving laws, licensing regulations, capital punishment, liquor laws, homosexuality and other sexual deviations, marriage and divorce laws, child abuse and adoption laws, the organization, operations, and finances of particular local governments, the services of these governments, and the developmental planning of particular states, cities, counties or regions. But such topics are not assigned to presidential commissions.

In general, however, presidential and royal commissions treat similar subjects. Yet royal commissions have, over the years, established a far better record than presidential commissions for the impact, usefulness and nonpolitical character of their advice. Since the early nineteenth century, royal commissions have been a major source of British social reform. Sir Cecil Thomas Carr, in *Concerning British Administrative Law,* wrote that the recommendations of Victorian commissions led to "a quick and quiet revolution in the laws of factories, poor relief, municipal corporations, prisons, public health, civil procedure, and . . . mitigation of savage

50

punishments." In *Parliamentary Government in England*, British political scientist Harold Laski wrote of the royal commission: "The aid that device has given to clarity in both policy and administration is literally beyond estimation." Felix Frankfurter, Supreme Court Justice, wrote in *The Public and Its Government:* "The history of British democracy might in considerable measure be written in terms of the history of successive Royal Commissions." No such statements could be made of presidential commissions.

Presidential and royal commissions have different symbolic positions within their systems of government. Royal commissions are created by the monarch, the head of state, and not by the Prime Minister, the head of the government; their powers are, at least in theory, derived from the disinterested prestige of the throne. (Admittedly, the monarch establishes royal commissions only because the Prime Minister and cabinet tell him to do so.) The powers of presidential commissions are derived from the often partisan position of the President. The Presidency combines the roles of head of state and head of government, and thus presidential commissions cannot be as nonpolitical as royal commissions. As instruments of the Presidency, presidential commissions are symbolically more responsible to the President than to the public. As instruments of the throne, royal commissions are symbolically more responsible to the public than to the Prime Minister or the cabinet.

Presidential and royal commissions have different legal positions within their systems of government. In *Guide to Decision: The Royal Commission*, published in 1965, and the only full-length study of the British institution in more than thirty years, Charles Hanser wrote that the royal commission "is not part of or subordinate to any other institution. It is not a committee responsible to a larger body; it has a legal status formally equal to that of the other primary institutions of the state, such as Parliament or Privy Council. . . . It does not advise any department, the cabinet, or even Parliament, therefore it is not subservient to any. It reports to the Crown itself." During the twentieth century, royal commissions have been appointed about as often as presidential commissions, but without the fluctuations in frequency which have characterized presidential commissions: no Prime Minister has been significantly more or less willing than any other to create royal commissions.

Presidential and royal commissions have different constitutional positions within their systems of government. The British government operates by means of the principle of fusion of powers: in theory, the monarch, Prime Minister, cabinet, and Parliament must work in agreement (although, in practice, the Prime Minister and cabinet are dominant). A royal commission operates in the name of the entire government, which therefore will be predisposed to accept the commission's recommendations.

The American government, on the other hand, separates powers: competition is encouraged between and within the executive, legislative, and judicial branches. In the American system, there is nothing comparable to the party discipline of the British system. A presidential commission operates, at most, only in the name of the executive branch. In America, there is no equivalent to the collective responsibility of the British Cabinet. A presidential commission may not be operating on behalf of the entire executive branch; when a commission goads, assesses, or investigates agencies, it represents only the Presidency, not the bureaucracy of the rest of the executive branch. Finally, a commission has to compete for the attention of the President. The entire constitutional and political position of a presidential commission is far more turbulent and insecure than that of a royal commission.

Presidential and royal commissions exist in different social and cultural environments. Hanser ascribes the success of the royal commission to "several acknowledged features of British life," which are "the public service orientation in higher education; the sense of public duty and the influence of the older aristocratic *noblesse oblige*; the high ranking given public life generally; the honor of being selected a Royal Commissioner." Of these four features, only the last is of comparable strength in the United States. As a result, British commissioners work harder than American ones, form a more cohesive group, and feel more responsible for their

52

recommendations. The enormity of their duties is willingly accepted, and they actually write most of their commission reports themselves.

Sir John Simon, a member of a 1929 Commission on Labour in India (then a Labour Member of Parliament, later Foreign Secretary, Home Secretary, Chancellor of the Exchequer, and Lord Chancellor), wrote in his memoirs, *Retrospect*, that his commission service "meant the complete abandonment of my practice at the Bar and the devotion of all my energies to an immense and labourious inquiry, which ended three years later." The same commission's chairman, Clement Attlee (then a Labour M.P., Prime Minister from 1945 to 1951, and later Earl Attlee), wrote in his memoirs, *As It Happened*, that he was hardly able to appear in the House of Commons because of the demands of his commission service. Hanser wrote that there "is no personal exploitation of the office of Royal Commissioner, no leaving the burden of actual work to an anonymous staff."

In contrast, Admiral Hyman Rickover, testifying before the House Committee on Governmental Operations, in 1959, described, with only slight exaggeration, the prevalent atmosphere of Defense Department committees, and his description applies as well to presidential commissions: "The members of [these committees] have no responsibility, but take the liberty of making recommendations and then running off somewhere else and getting on some other committees on another subject and making some more recommendations. . . . They come around, talk for a little while, make a recommendation, and go back to playing golf or whatever else they do. . . . They have a paper responsibility to make a certain recommendation, but once they make that recommendation, they cheerfully disband and go on and get on some other committee."

Presidential and royal commissions differ in their composition. The tendency toward multiple service by commissioners is weaker in Britain, perhaps because commission service is more demanding there. As stated in Chapter 3, at least 10 per cent of the membership of any presidential commission is likely to serve again or to have served before

4 ★

on another commission, but Hanser gives figures which suggest that the comparable British figure is less than 4 per cent. More important, royal commissions, because they are smaller than presidential commissions, can work harder. Hanser states that the average size of twentieth-century royal commissions has been ten members; of President Johnson's twenty commissions, only two—the Warren and D.C. Crime Commissions—had fewer than ten members. England is smaller and more homogeneous than the United States, and the principle of interest-group liberalism is much weaker. Royal commissions can be smaller than presidential commissions because they need not represent as many regional, religious, ethnic, and racial groups.

Royal and presidential commissions also differ in their operations. The pressure for a consensus is not as strong on a royal commission. No recent presidential commission has issued a minority report, but Hanser states that 25 per cent of the royal commissions of the twentieth century have issued such reports. He adds that divided royal commissions were likely to be those few commissions (he estimates about one-sixth) in which particular efforts had been made to represent competing interests—that is, those commissions most like presidential commissions. Presidential commissioners apparently view a minority report as an embarrassment that might cause them unwanted work. Royal commissioners, on the other hand, view a minority report as a necessary and desirable way to represent their positions, and several of these reports, such as the 1909 Minority Report of the Poor Law Commission, have been more influential than the accompanying majority reports. Royal commissioners feel more strongly about their efforts than presidential commissioners, and are less willing to arrange compromises among themselves.

There are other operational differences between presidential and royal commissions. The executive director of a royal commission is usually a senior civil servant instead of a political lawyer or an academic. The staffs of royal commissions contain fewer lawyers. The costs of royal and presidential commissions are comparable, but royal commissions

54

have unlimited budgets. They also have no deadlines; although few operate for more than three years, royal commissions conclude their operations when they wish. Unlike presidential commissions, they do not have to depend on their appointers for release of their report; they have a uniform release procedure. They do not have to devote much effort to public relations in order to get attention. A Prime Minister cannot delay release because he does not like a report, and he cannot thrust a report on the public because it pleases him. Thus, again unlike presidential commissions, royal commissions are more responsible to the public than to their appointers.

The resemblances between presidential and royal commissions are clearly superficial. Their symbolic, legal, constitutional, environmental, compositional, and operational differences are much more important than their similarities. All the differences make royal commissions less narrowly political and more concerned with substantive, long-range policy than presidential commissions. Royal commissions can make more intensive examinations of their topics than presidential commissions because they can afford a wider perspective. All the differences between presidential and royal commissions make the recommendations of presidential commissions less weighty and less influential than those of royal commissions.

9. CONCLUSION: A NEED FOR IMPROVEMENT

Presidential commissions have many flaws. In general, they are too political. Their rosters are often too large, contain too many repeating members, and consistently underrepresent important groups. Their memberships are often inattentive and uncohesive. Their research is rushed and inadequate. They come to consensus conclusions which avoid many of the questions that caused the creation of a commission in the first place. Their reports are released haphazardly. Their most original recommendations are the ones most likely to be shelved. Their members and staffs rarely make a serious effort to convince their constituencies of the merits of their recommendations. All the defects that Epstein condemned in the Warren Commission may be found in other commissions. No commission report, not even that of the much vilified Warren Commission, is incompetent, negligent, or rash, but few, if any, are brilliant.

A case could be made for doing away with commissions entirely. But, despite their flaws, commissions remain the most effective mechanism in the American government for providing the President publicly with disinterested, prestigious advice. They can, in principle, perform great services for the President and the public, but too often they have not fulfilled their potential. The money spent on them has by no means been wasted, but they can be improved, easily and inexpensively. Of the recommendations below, all but the final and most important one require only informal action by the President, his assistants, commissioners, or staff members.

Fewer commissions should be appointed in the future. In the period 1963-1968, President Kennedy and President Johnson created twenty-two commissions, an average of nearly four commissions a year; and in his first year in office, President Nixon created or announced plans for five. Such frequent use of commissions tends to devalue them. Two commissions a year, which is approximately the over-all, twentieth-century rate of appointment of presidential commissions, as well as the rate of appointment of royal commissions, seems reasonable.

56

Between 1963 and 1968, President Johnson appointed three commissions of intense interest to the public, and this pace also seems too rapid. Such commissions, as well as other commissions to a lesser extent, tend to produce frustration by arousing expectations which are not met, or which cannot be met. The members of President Nixon's staff agree; they are aware that the commissions which received the most publicity did not help President Johnson (or President Nixon) in any way. When the Eisenhower Commission released its report, commissioner A. Leon Higginbotham called independently for a moratorium on commissions "to probe the causes of racism, or poverty, or crime, or the urban crisis" and added that there had already been too much study and too little action. Kenneth Clark, a black psychologist, told the Kerner Commission hearings that commissions to investigate riots were "a kind of Alice in Wonderland—with the same moving picture shown over and over again, the same analysis, the same recommendations, and the same inaction." The commission agreed and, almost plaintively, cited his testimony at the conclusion of its report.

Such criticism is valid but, on political *and* moral grounds, if a President cannot and will not attack a broad social problem, he should not appoint a commission, especially a highly publicized commission, to study it. Such a commission will either publicly reveal his inability and unwillingness, or evade them unconvincingly. Prime Ministers rarely appoint such commissions (there have been no royal commissions on Britain's racial problems, or on the Northern Ireland disorders), and there is no reason why Presidents should make the mistake of appointing them. Commissions should be more than sops. A President should appoint only one highly publicized commission, at most, during each four-year term, and he should appoint it only if he is willing and able to implement its recommendations.

The more effective commissions, in both Britain and the United States, are the smaller ones. Such commissions meet more often, work harder, work out their differences more constructively, and produce a report more rapidly than the large commissions. (President Nixon's All-Volunteer Armed

Force Commission, the only commission he has yet appointed, had fifteen members, a fairly small number for an American commission and a sign that important advice was expected from the group.) Commissions should be as small as possible.

If commissions are to be small, not all the constituencies which have been represented in the past can continue to be represented. Interest-group liberalism, in itself a reasonable principle, can be carried to the point where it hinders the efficiency of a commission by liberally representing comparatively unimportant interest groups. It is questionable whether the customary representation of such marginal constituencies as the media, agriculture, local government, and previous administrations has actually added anything to commissions over the years. Some constituencies are important, specific representatives of them have made useful contributions, and they should be represented on commissions whose topic is of particular interest to them. But they need not be represented on every commission. Similarly, a friend of the President need not have a reserved place on a commission roster; a President generally has enough control over a commission and its work anyway, and need not risk accusations of cronyism. Past commissions have contained too many token representatives, and future commission rosters should, wherever possible, dispense with them. Future rosters should also be shortened by including more commissioners who combine constituencies.

At the same time, significant American constituencies which have been consistently underrepresented in the past—young people, women, the genuinely poor, and educators below the college level are all good examples—should receive greater representation, in legitimate accordance with the principle of interest-group liberalism. Even more important, every commission should include at least one member who has had recent first-hand experience with the commission's topic. Present commissioners, because they are so established, have been sheltered from such experience, no matter what constituencies they nominally represent. There is no evidence that any riot commissioner has ever been a rioter, the target of a riot, or even in a riot; that any medical commissioner has ever lacked medical care; that any draft commissioner has been drafted or has drafted anyone in the last fifteen years.

If a commissioner has had any previous experience with his commission's topic, it is likely to have been bureaucratic or intellectual rather than personal. Staff members and consultants are equally likely to lack such personal experience. A commission on a pressing social problem, in effect, excludes those who have had any real contact with it. As a result, a commission, despite all its work, only rarely comes to grips with the realities of its subject, and its recommendations are always produced by an unreal, overly detached consensus. The appointment of commissioners, as well as the recruitment of staff members and consultants, who have genuine experience with the subjects of their commissions will be difficult, and will lead to clashes. However, such appointment and recruitment are essential if commission advice is to represent more than a politically facile, but ultimately ineffectual, pragmatism. Every future commission roster should contain at least one member who represents experience instead of eminence, whose constituency is reality.

Future rosters should contain fewer repeating members. Multiple appointments are not desirable; commission advice is seriously compromised if it appears to come from an incestuous group. Multiple appointments are not necessary; many eminent and otherwise qualified men and women have never been appointed to a commission. Commissioners who have served with distinction on one commission should still be considered for appointment to another, as they are in Britain, but in the past repeated appointments have not necessarily been the result of prior outstanding performance; in the future they should be. No person should be appointed to more than two commissions. No commissioner should be appointed to a second commission until some time—say, three years—after his first commission has reported. No commission chairman should be appointed to a second commission. All these recommendations should apply across all changes in administrations. Every effort should be made to reduce the percentage of commission members who have served before and will serve again from the present level, well in excess of 10 per cent, to about 5 per cent, a percentage comparable to that of royal commissions. Commission appointments should allow commissions to draw on as many opinions as possible.

The presidential staff should make clear to commissioners that they must, in the future, be more attentive to commission work. Attentiveness should be considered a condition of appointment; if a prospective commissioner cannot comply, then he should not be offered appointment. Commissioners should be made to understand that their work is vitally important, must not be undertaken lightly, will demand their closest attention, and may require that they drop other commitments.

The workload of commissions should be increased commensurately. Most past commissions have not met two days a month, but every future commission should meet at least four days a month. Every commissioner should be required to attend almost all the meetings and hearings of his commission. Every commissioner should be required to contribute to the final report a statement of his own findings, including his points of agreement and disagreement with the report of the commission as a whole. Such a required statement might reduce the pressures of interest-group liberalism by encouraging *de facto* minority reports and discouraging the evasive, useless expressions of consensus too often contained in the reports of presidential commissions. Not all commissioners need work full-time, but if, say, a third did and if this third were representative of the entire roster, the results might be surprisingly beneficial. All these work requirements would bind commissions, make them as cohesive as royal commissions, and stimulate commissioners to rouse their constituencies in support of their recommendations.

The deadlines imposed on commissions should be relaxed. The present tight deadlines—usually eighteen months or less—hinder the recruitment of good staff members, and also mean that lawyers and government employees are more

60

likely to be hired than writers or academics. The deadlines force the executive director to be no more than an administrator and hinder the performance of competent, pertinent research, both by the consultants and the staff members. The deadlines also mean that commission reports are always written hurriedly. Most commissions should have at least two years to conduct their work. Some commissions might, like royal commissions, have no deadlines. Those technical commissions which do not need such distant deadlines can probably finish their work in eight months, and the work of such commissions might well be handled better by executive branch committees. Giving most commissions distant deadlines would allow commissioners to write their own reports. More journalists and other staff members with literary skills would be able to assist in drafting reports. Many academics now hired as consultants could become full-time staff members. The fact that the two-year life of a commission might span administrations need not be a problem; as discussed in previous chapters, Presidents are often willing to take the advice of a commission appointed by a predecessor.

The writing in commission reports needs considerable improvement. Most are not read closely, and for good reason. More distant deadlines might produce better, more intelligible writing by people with literary experience. Most reports should be shorter; 30,000 words is a reasonable upper limit (the Kerner report was about 200,000). Some could be as short as 5,000 words.

The format of commission reports is usually confusing. The reports present so many detailed recommendations that the reader is likely to get lost in the details and to have little idea which recommendations the commission considers most important. The surfeit of recommendations without priorities forces even the knowledgeable reader to skim commission reports. This skimming has important political consequences: when reading the report, the President, his assistants, men in the upper ranks of agencies, and the press often lose sight of the organization of the entire report and focus, quite haphazardly, on specific recommendations. Nathan Glazer described a preinaugural task force meeting at which William

61

Gorham, President of the Urban Institute, emphasized the random reading of task force and commission reports: "[Gorham] told the task force arguing about fine points in its presentation, that . . . the secretary or whoever this goes to will pick up a piece here and a piece there, because this looks good and that looks possible. The proposals that eventually get sent up to the President or to Congress will look nothing like the rounded harmonious product you think you are putting together. So humbled, the task force returned to work."

Future commission members and writers of commission reports should have a similar attitude. Commission reports should be shorter, should have fewer detailed recommendations, and should explicitly state and justify the priorities among recommendations, or packages of recommendations. Whenever appropriate, commission reports should include sample drafts of Executive Orders, legislation, or other action documents carrying out commission recommendations. The reports of presidential commissions, like those of royal commissions, should estimate the costs of their recommendations and should suggest means of meeting these costs. Some presidential commissions might follow the procedure of some royal commissions by writing two reports: a technical report for the sophisticated reader and a popular report for the less knowledgeable reader.

Commissions need not publish the supplementary volumes of technical papers by consultants. These volumes may sometimes be necessary background for the commission's own work, but the government should not have to bear the cost of publishing several thousand copies. The authors of the best material in these volumes can publish their work elsewhere, where publication can be more visible, and the worst material forgotten. Not publishing these supplementary volumes would save money, as would not publishing transcripts of hearings. In exceptional cases, such as the Warren Commission, where this material is likely to be read, supplementary volumes and hearing transcripts should be published, but in general such material need only be available in government archives. No one reads it, and there is no reason to spend public money publishing and distributing it.

Commissions' public relations activities should give them a chance to defend their own interests more effectively. Presidential commissions should have a uniform release procedure similar to that of royal commissions. Commission work which is outstandingly important and timely should be released to the public well before the commission's deadline, thus calling public attention to the commission. The early release of some of the Eisenhower Commission's research, particularly the Walker Report, set a useful precedent which other commissions can and should pursue.

The Eisenhower Commission's early release of separate statements of its position on specific issues set an equally commendable public relations precedent. These statements also seemed to relieve the pressures for consensus within the group: two of the statements were not unanimous. A July 1969 statement recommending that a federal law be enacted establishing standards for individual hand gun ownership was publicly opposed by four of the thirteen commissioners. A December 1969 statement which, surprisingly, condemned civil disobedience as leading to anarchy was opposed by six commissioners. Without these statements, the commission's final report might not have been unanimous, but, as royal commissioners know, unanimity and consensus are by no means desirable in every aspect of commission work. Every effort should be made to encourage constructive dissent and debate within commissions. In fact, divided position statements, as well as divided final reports, should not be discouraged: they should be encouraged.

Finally, and most important, all those connected with commissions should reconsider to whom commissions are responsible, and to whom they should be responsible. Commissions advise the President and, in principle, report only to him. However, this arrangement has led to genuine abuses, especially the narrowly political use by the President of a mechanism which is ostensibly out of politics and which functions best when it actually *is* apolitical. Under the present arrangement, Congress, which must pass on commission recommendations, and the public, in whose interest commissions are presumably appointed, have no control over commissions. They should have such control.

The present arrangement might be modified, perhaps on an experimental basis, by having the President and Congress jointly create commissions which would report directly to the public without having to wait for presidential or congressional approval. The President and Congress would informally agree on a commission's topic. They would each appoint one-half the members, none of whom could come from the executive or legislative branches. Half the cost of the commission would be met by the various White House Funds, half by congressional appropriation. Also, the President, Congress, and the Supreme Court could jointly create commissions which also would report directly to the public. The President, Congress, and the Court would informally agree on the commission's topic and each would appoint one-third of the members, none of whom could come from the executive, legislative, or judicial branches. A third of the cost would be met by the White House, a third by Congress, and a third by the Court.

Commissions created in either of these ways would not be presidential commissions; they would be national commissions. They would have the same rank as the President, the Senate, the House, or the Supreme Court. Without costing more than presidential commissions and without seriously compromising the American constitutional principle of separation of powers, their legal and symbolic positions would be comparable to those of royal commissions, and their advice, to the government and to the public, would have a comparable influence. They might also be able to probe the heretofore unexamined areas of foreign policy and military strategy. The creation of such national commissions, which would probably require a statutory base, should be seriously considered.

Commissions have, in the past, involved far more prestige and publicity than substance, and several commissions can only be described as extravaganzas. These defects can be corrected; the alternative to such correction is continued misuse of a valuable institution. To give commissions substance, to make them more than an impressive gimmick of the Presidency, and, most important, to make them operate solely in the public interest, rigorous recommendations such as those above should be adopted.

APPENDIX 1: PRESIDENTIAL COMMISSIONS, 1945-1970

President	Presidential Commission	Announced	Reporte•
Truman	Universal Training	1946	1947
	Higher Education	1946	1947
	Employee Loyalty	1946	1947
	Air Policy	1947	1948
	The Organization of the Executive Branch of the Government (First Hoover Commission)	1947	1949
	Water Resources Policy	1949	1950
	Migratory Labor	1950	1951
	Airports	1951	1952
	Health Needs of the Nation	1951	1952
	Materials Policy	1951	1952
	Immigration and Naturalization	1952	1953
Eisenhower	Foreign Economic Policy	1953	1954
	The Organization of the Executive Branch of the Government (Second Hoover Commission)	1953	1955
	Veterans' Pensions	1955	1956
	National Goals	1960	1960
Kennedy	Campaign Costs	1961	1962
	Status of Women	1961	1963
	Narcotics and Drug Abuse	1963	1963
	Registration and Voting Participation	1963	1963 (to Johnso
Johnson	The Assassination of President Kennedy (Warren Commission)	1963	1964
	Heart Disease, Cancer and Stroke	1963	1964

66

President	Presidential Commission	Announced	Reported
Johnson	Technology, Automation and Economic Progress	1964	1966
	Urban Problems	1965	1969
	The Patent System	1965	1966
	Crime in the District of Columbia	1965	1966
	Law Enforcement and Administration of Justice	1965	1967
	Food and Fiber	1965	1967
	Health Manpower	1966	1967
	Marine Science, Engineering and Resources	1966	1968
	Selective Service	1966	1967
	Libraries	1966	1967
	Rural Poverty	1966	1967
	Urban Housing	1967	1968
	Budget Concepts	1967	1967
	Health Facilities	1967	1968
	Postal Organization	1967	1968
	Civil Disorders (Kerner Commission)	1967	1968
	Income Maintenance Programs	1968	1969 (to Nixon)
	The Causes and Prevention of Violence (Eisenhower Commission)	1968	1969 (to Nixon)
Nixon	An All-Volunteer Armed Force	1969	1970
	Self Government for the District of Columbia	1969	not yet appointed
	World Trade	1969	not yet appointed
	Population Growth and the American Future	1969	not yet appointed
	School Finance	1970	not yet appointed

APPENDIX 2: THE MEMBERS OF THE SELECTIVE SERVICE COMMISSION*

Name	Position at Appointment	Other Information†
Kingman Brewster	President, Yale University	47; lawyer; professor of law at Harvard, 1953-61; provost and professor of law at Yale, 1961-63; see Appendix 4
Thomas S. Gates	Chairman of Board, Morgan Guaranty Trust Company, New York	60; Republican; Navy Secretary, 1957-59; Defense Undersecretary, 1959; Defense Secretary, 1959-61; see Appendix 4
Oveta Culp Hobby (Mrs. William P. Hobby)	Editor and Chairman of Board, *Houston Post*	61; Republican; HEW Secretary, 1953-55
Anna Rosenberg Hoffman (Mrs. Paul Hoffman)	President, Rosenberg Associates, a New York public and industrial relations consulting firm	64; Democrat; Jewish; Assistant Defense Secretary, 1950-53; born in Hungary; also on President Truman's Universal Training Commission; see Appendix 3
Paul J. Jennings	President, International Union of Electrical, Radio and Machine Workers	Age not available; lives in Washington
John H. Johnson	Publisher of *Ebony, Tan*, and *Jet*	48; editor; black; lives in Chicago; see Appendix 4
Vernon E. Jordan	Director, Voter Education Project, Southern Regional Council	31; black; lawyer; lives in Atlanta
Daniel M. Luevano	Director, Western Region, Office of Economic Opportunity	Age not available; Mexican descent; lives in San Francisco
Burke Marshall (Chairman)	Vice President and General Counsel, IBM	44; Democrat; lawyer; Assistant Attorney General, 1961-65; lives in New York
John A. McCone	President, Joshua Hendy Corporation, a ship-building firm	64; Republican; Irish descent; Catholic; Atomic Energy Commission Chairman, 1958-60; CIA Director, 1961-65; also on President Truman's Air Policy Commission; lives in Los Angeles; see Appendix 4
James H. McCrocklin	President, Southwest Texas State College (President Johnson's alma mater)	43; Democrat; political scientist; professor and department chairman, Texas College of Arts and Industries, 1957-64; HEW Undersecretary, 1967

* Sources for Appendices: Commission reports, *Who's Who in America*, and various professional directories.

† Age in 1966, year of appointment.

Name	Position at Appointment	Other Information
John Courtney Murray	Professor of Theology, Woodstock College	Age not available; Jesuit; lives in Maryland; written on conscientious objection
Jeanne L. Noble	Professor of Education, Center for Human Relations Studies, New York University	Age not available; black; Vice President, National Council of Negro Women; see Appendix 3
George E. Reedy	President, Struthers Research and Development Corporation, a marine research firm	49; Democrat; President's Press Secretary, 1964-65; lives in Texas; see Appendix 3
David Monroe Shoup	General, U.S. Marine Corps (ret.)	62; Commandant, U.S. Marine Corps, 1960-63; lives in Virginia
Fiorindo A. Simeone	Professor of Surgery, Western Reserve University Medical School	58; born in Italy; Catholic; physician; now at Brown University
James A. Suffridge	International President, Retail Clerks International Association	57; Republican; lives in Washington
Frank S. Syzmanski	Judge of Probate, Detroit	Age not available; Democrat; Polish descent; Catholic; lawyer
Luther L. Terry	Vice President for Medical Affairs, University of Pennsylvania	55; physician; heart specialist; U.S. Surgeon General, 1961-65; lives in Philadelphia
Warren G. Woodward	Vice President, American Airlines	Age not available; lives in Texas

APPENDIX 3: MEMBERS OF THREE COMMISSIONS, 1950-1970

Name	Commissions*	Position at Latest Appointment	Other Information†
Alfred M. Gruenther[1]	National Goals; Heart Disease, Cancer and Stroke; All-Volunteer Armed Force	General, U.S. Army (ret.)	70; Supreme Allied Commander in Europe, 1953-56; lives in Washington
Anna Rosenberg Hoffman[2] (Mrs. Paul Hoffman)	Technology; Selective Service; Income Maintenance	President, Rosenberg Associates, New York public and industrial relations consulting firm	66; Democrat; Jewish; Assistant Defense Secretary, 1950-53; born in Hungary; also on President Truman's Universal Training Commission
Leon Jaworski[2]	Law Enforcement; Marine Science; Eisenhower	Partner, Houston law firm of Fulbright, Crooker, Freeman, Bates and Jaworski	63; Democrat; lawyer
George Meany[1]	National Goals; Postal Organization; Urban Housing	President, AFL-CIO	73; Democrat; Catholic; lives in Washington
J. Irwin Miller[2]	Postal Organization; Urban Housing; Health Manpower (chairman)	Chairman of Board, Cummins Engine Company	58; Republican; President, National Council of Churches, 1960-63; lives in Indianapolis
George E. Reedy[2]	Selective Service; Marine Science; Income Maintenance	President, Struthers Research and Development Corporation, a marine research firm	51; Democrat; President's Press Secretary, 1964-65; lives in Texas
Whitney M. Young[2]	Technology; Law Enforcement; Urban Housing	Executive Director, National Urban League	46; black; lives in New York

* None of the commissioners served only on commissions appointed by Republican Presidents, and none served on commissions appointed by more than one Democratic President.

† Age in year of latest appointment.

[1] Served on commissions appointed by Presidents of both parties.

[2] Served only on commissions appointed by President Johnson.

APPENDIX 4: MEMBERS OF TWO COMMISSIONS, 1950-1970

Name	Commissions	Position at Latest Appointment	Other Information*
Joseph A. Beirne[2]	Technology; Health Manpower	President, Communications Workers of America	55; Democrat; Irish descent; Catholic; lives in Washington
Sherwood O. Berg[2]	Food and Fiber (chairman); Income Maintenance	Dean, Institute of Agriculture, University of Minnesota	49; agricultural economist; professor and department chairman, University of Minnesota, 1957-63
Hale Boggs[2]	Warren; Eisenhower	Louisiana Representative; Assistant Majority Leader	54; Democrat; Catholic; lawyer
Kingman Brewster[2]	Law Enforcement; Selective Service	President, Yale University	47; lawyer; professor of law, Harvard, 1953-61; provost and professor of law, Yale, 1961-63
Mary I. Bunting[3] (Mrs. Henry Bunting)	Status of Women; Health Manpower	President, Radcliffe College	56; bacteriologist; dean at Rutgers, 1955-59
Gaylord Freeman[2]	Health Manpower; Urban Housing	Vice Chairman, First National Bank of Chicago	57; now Chairman, First National Bank of Chicago
Thomas S. Gates[1]	Selective Service; All-Volunteer Armed Force (chairman)	Chairman of Executive Committee, Morgan Guaranty Trust Company, New York	63; Republican; Navy Secretary, 1957-59; Defense Undersecretary, 1959; Defense Secretary, 1959-61
Crawford A. Greenewalt[4]	National Goals; All-Volunteer Armed Force	Chairman of Finance Committee, E.I. duPont Company	67; chemical engineer; duPont Vice President, 1946-48, President, 1948-62; Chairman of Board, 1962-67; lives in Wilmington, Delaware
John H. Johnson[2]	Selective Service; Urban Housing	Publisher of *Ebony*, *Tan*, and *Jet*	49; black; lives in Chicago

*Age in year of latest appointment.

Name	Commissions	Position at Latest Appointment	Other Information
John A. McCone[2]	Selective Service; Urban Housing	President; Joshua Hendy Corporation, a ship-building firm	65; Republican; Irish descent; Catholic; AEC Chairman, 1958-60; CIA Director, 1961-65; also o President Truman's Air Policy Commission; lives in Los Angeles
William M. McCulloch[2]	Kerner; Eisenhower	Ohio Representative	67; Republican; lawyer
W. Beverly Murphy[2]	Food and Fiber; Postal Organization	President, Campbell Soup Company	62; Republican; lives in Philadelphia
Jeanne L. Noble[1]	Selective Service; All-Volunteer Armed Force	Professor of Education, Center for Human Relations Studies, New York University	Age not available; black; Vice President, National Council of Negro Women
Henry Huntt Ransom[2]	Libraries; Patent System (co-chairman)	Chancellor, University of Texas System	58; historian; professor, University of Texas, 194 present; Dean, University Texas, 1954-57; Vice President and Provost, University of Texas, 195 60; President, University Texas, 1960-61; lives in Austin, Texas
Walter Reuther[2]	Technology; Urban Housing	President, United Auto Workers of America	60; lives in Detroit
William P. Rogers[2]	Law Enforcement; D.C. Crime	Partner, New York and Washington law firm of Royall, Koegel and Rogers	52; Republican; lawyer; Deputy Attorney Genera 1953-57; Attorney Gene 1957-61; now Secretary of State
Howard Rusk[3]	Health Needs; Heart Disease, Cancer and Stroke	Professor of Rehabilitation, New York University Medical School; New York Times health columnist	62; physician
J. Julian Samora[2]	Rural Poverty; Income Maintenance	Professor of Sociology, Notre Dame	48; Mexican-American descent; Catholic

ne	Commissions	Position at Latest Appointment	Other Information
ert ow[2]	Technology; Income Maintenance	Professor of Economics, Massachusetts Institute of Technology	44; Jewish
ert rey[1]	Second Hoover Commission; Law Enforcement	Former Dean, Southern Methodist University Law School, 1947-59	72; lawyer; lives in Dallas
id livan[2]	Health Facilities; Income Maintenance	President, Building Service Employees International Union	64; Catholic; born in Ireland; lives in New York
rles B. rnton[2]	Patent System; Kerner	President and Chairman of Board, Litton Industries	55; Vice President, Hughes Tool Company, 1948-53; lives in Los Angeles
mas J. tson[2]	Technology; Income Maintenance	Chairman of Board, IBM	54; President, IBM, 1952-61; lives in New York
n H. eeler[2]	Food and Fiber; Urban Housing	President, Mechanics and Farmers Bank, Durham, North Carolina	59; black; lawyer; lives in Durham
y Wilkins[1]	Kerner; All-Volunteer Armed Force	Executive Director, NAACP	68; black; lives in New York

ge in year of latest appointment.

erved on commissions appointed by Presidents of both parties.

erved only on commissions appointed by President Johnson.

erved only on commissions appointed by more than one Democratic President.

erved only on commissions appointed by Republican Presidents.